The White Room

The White Room

Poems by

Cynthia Pitman

Cover design by Shay Culligan

Cover photograph by Daria Nepriakhina
(unsplash.com)

ISBN: 978-1-952326-00-4

Kelsay Books Inc.

kelsaybooks.com

502 S 1040 E, A119
American Fork, Utah 84003

To Tom, Rebecca, and Eric

Acknowledgments

Literary Yard: "Amalgamated Memories"
Adelaide Magazine: "Ascension"
Mused: Bella Online: "#BelieveAllWomen"
Adelaide Magazine: "Breakdown of the Bicameral Mind"
Amethyst Review: "Prophet"
Amethyst Review: "The Coming of Spring"
Vita Brevis: "Cornered"
Amethyst Review: "The Dance of the Seven Veils"
Vita Brevis: "Excavation of a Dream"
Leaves of Ink: "Flashbacks of a Survivor"
Literary Yard: "The Girls of Summer"
Amethyst Review: "My Grandmother's Crystal"
Leaves of Ink: "Hurricane"
Adelaide Literary Review: "Inclination"
Leaves of Ink: "Lamentation: A Lullaby"
Literary Yard: "Laws of Physics"
Vita Brevis: "The Dark Side of the Moon"
Leaves of Ink: "Melancholy Comfort"
Leaves of Ink: "Now We Cry"
Leaves of Ink: "Opening Day"
Literary Yard: "The Garden"
Literary Yard: "The Painted Bison"
Adelaide Magazine: "Penetrating Secrets"
Leaves of Ink: "Phantom Pains"
Amethyst Review: "The Coming of Spring"
Leaves of Ink: "Red Water"
Literary Yard: "Revelation"
Leaves of Ink: "Revival"
Third Wednesday: "Solo"
Leaves of Ink: "Song of Mourning"
Leaves of Ink: "Silent Star"
Literary Yard: "Still Life in Lies"

Leaves of Ink: "Storm Warning"
Three Line Poetry: "Tidal Waltz"
Amethyst Review: "Trinity"
Vita Brevis: "Where I Come From"
Right Hand Pointing: "The White Room"
Ekphrastic Review: "Witch Hunt"
Literary Yard: "Woman Working: Trilogy"
Postcard Poems and Prose: "The Wooden Swing"

Contents

Excavation of a Dream	13
Solo	14
Cornered	15
The Girls of Summer	16
The Birth of Fall	17
The Garden	18
Red Water	19
The Coming of Spring	20
Storm Warning	21
Hurricane	22
Penetrating Secrets	23
Now We Cry	25
The Dance of Love	26
The Dark Side of the Moon	27
The Butterfly Effect	28
Still Life in Lies	29
Stunt Double	30
The Wooden Swing	31
The Laws of Physics	32
Supplication	33
Phantom Pains	34
Lamentation: A Lullaby	35
The White Room	36
Grief	37
Melancholy Comfort	38
Silent Star	39
Revival	40
Song of Mourning	41
Revelation	42
Amalgamated Memories	43
Flashbacks of a Survivor	44
Hallucination	45
How to Photoshop a Background	46
Kaleidoscope	47

The Prophet   48
The Breakdown of the Bicameral Mind   49
The Shape of Shadows   50
Being and Nothingness   51
The Delusion of Hope   52
An Autobiography of Dying   54
After It's Over   56
Purgatory   57
Ascension   58
Trinity   59
Inclination   61
The Archaeology of Ruins   62
The Painted Bison   64
When the Hurly-Burly's Done   66
#BelieveAllWomen   67
Woman Resolute   68
Witch Hunt: Salem   69
Working Woman Trilogy   71
The Dance of the Seven Veils   74
Tidal Waltz   76
Masquerade   77
When I Was a Child   78
Front Porch Concerto   79
Where I Come From, We Call Them   80
"Lightning Bugs"   80
Pirouette   81
Opening Day   82

Excavation of a Dream

I sit at the table, elbow up,
propping my chin in my hand in front of my laptop.
My impatient accomplice whirs and whirs,
trying to stir me back to work.
But I won't go.
Instead, I lean into my daydreams.
I gaze outside.
So many layers separate me from the world.
The soft-pink rose-lace curtains that I chose
to mimic my grandmother's house hang light,
overlaying a window with fifteen panes—
all of the panes etched with roses
sunlight-sifted through the curtains.
Beyond is the shade from the trees,
light and dark gray on the asphalt.
Someone must have come along
and spilled white paint on the shade,
for here and there blots of white mottle it.
They move with the wind.
The grass lies green,
lime-green or forest green,
its color decided by the shade.
Below is the dirt.
Were I to dig, the warm topsoil would be tight,
hardened by the sun.
But were I to dig deep, it would become cold and fresh,
fed by spring water bubbling in the earth.
Clumps of rich dirt would cling to my hands.
I return to my laptop.
I dig deep and dirty my hands
with fertile words.

Solo

She sits cross-legged on the bed,
a slip of a girl.
Elbows bent, lips pursed,
she holds up a flute
and marks time
to the steady rhythm
of the stately metronome
standing straight and proud
on her nightstand.
She whispers a secret to the flute,
and its first notes
float in the air,
mystical gaslight in the fog.
Though measured and metered,
captured and welded
to dark bars of five lines,
they are, at the same time,
free to wander.
They drift into the ears
of those who listen for them,
then they drift away again.
The notes are,
and will always be,
vagabonds, loose in the world,
their travels mapped
by the will of a secret.

Cornered

A hapless mouse
has set up housekeeping
in the kitchen flour bin.
He gnawed on the rotting drawer-front
until he could let himself in,
then settled in the corner,
secure from the cold.
I think it would be fine, and good, and noble
if I, too, were to land-grab
a flour bin somewhere
and stake out my territory—
not to escape the cold,
but to escape the smothering heat
that radiates from this stove.
I would powder myself in soft white flour,
then run out wild and ransack the snow.

The Girls of Summer

Splayed on striped towels,
strapped tight in polka-dot bikinis
gritty with sand,
sweating from the sweltering heat
and burning a crispy-crust red
from the hot beach light
of the white-bright sky,
we lined up side-by-side,
one after another,
as if skewered over
a Fourth of July barbecue grill,
seeking the bestowal
of summer-brown beauty
as we worshiped our idol,
the Sun,
never noticing that quick, cold shiver,
never knowing that someday soon,
soon,
our Sun would set,
taking our summers forever with it,
leaving our white skies dark
and our young, tanned skin
old and leathered hides.

The Birth of Fall

The day hangs gray from the opalescent sky.
Silver-shaded clouds roof the world below
that now rests in relief from the stark sunshine.
The scorching heat has finally released
the air beneath,
absolving it of the penance it pays
to the burning star.
Now we can breathe in the alabaster embrace
of the cool wind's caress
that soothes us with its grace.

The Garden

Outside the window's smudged, cracked pane
remain a few red-flushed flowers
struggling in terra cotta window boxes.
They shed their yellowed leaves
onto the dry dirt below.
Their spindly stems stand tall,
bearing the last of their shrunken blossoms—
more berries now than blossoms
to our eyes that strain to see,
an unlikely forbidden fruit in this dying Eden.
We watch a lone chameleon
dart through the dead-leaved dirt
to escape the slaughter of the innocents
that strips the dying flowers from their stems.

Red Water

Part of the sleet was comfortable,
a familiar foe.
Its slanted needles, the spit of the sky,
jabbed our winter coats
with a sense of purpose.
Coming fast and determined,
the icy spikes failed to pierce
the thick wool coats we wore as armor.
For that, we cheered, reveling in victory
over our old foe's attack,
knowing our snowsuits
and our water-proof boots
would keep us safe—
all but the face.
We tried to look down but could only look up,
frozen in awe at the sharp-shaped water
sending down pain so constant and pure,
it bloodied our eyes wide open.

The Coming of Spring

Green gardenia bushes
line the butter-cream wall,
tended by a fountain goddess
standing tall on terra-cotta tiles
graced by painted fleurs de lis.
The still bushes await the spring,
when they will bear new leaves
and bring forth velvet white blossoms
that will saturate the air with sultry perfume.
We wait, too, for the coming rejuvenation
after winter blows away,
when we will stagger and teeter,
inebriate of our sodden senses.

Storm Warning

It's coming. I know.
The wind chimes warn me.
No rain. Not yet.
Only the growing wind,
bending branches.
A few straggling strips of bark
dance down the street,
a quick dance, a two-step,
marked with short stops.
A stick or two of spindly
dry limbs drag behind
at a slower clip,
keeping low to the ground.
Slate-gray shadows billow and follow them,
footprints of the clouds.
Soon they will thicken,
gathering ferocity from the electricity
that sparks the sky.
Then the burgeoning raindrops
will begin to   plop   plop   plop,
pocking the shadows
that swell with menace.
It's coming.
It's coming.
I know.
The wind chimes toll.
They toll for me.

Hurricane

The east side brushed by us.
A lot of rain came down, that's all.
It wasn't long until the sun came out,
shining on the long, wide, wet trail
left in the wake of the sweep of the storm.
I made a cup of tea, hot and sweet,
and walked out with it onto the front porch.
Everything everywhere was wet and shining:
the green of the trees,
the gray of the asphalt road,
even the dusty-red brick of the porch.
I lifted my head to look at the sky,
radiant in its cobalt blue.
Only two hundred miles away,
people were pulling their dead
from flooded streets.

Penetrating Secrets

With all your science, can you tell how it is
and whence it is that light comes into the soul?
                                        —Henry David Thoreau

No more need to wonder
why the sweltering heat of the wind
blows across the burning blacktop
of the splitting streets,
melting the thick tar pitch into a sticky cohesion,

or why the tornadoes gyre dry, raw terror
across the limitless prairies,
felling and flattening the homes, the trees, the animals
and the people,

or why the ocean's cryptic creatures
dwell deep in darkness,
adorned with rich jewel tones
that will never be seen,

or why the flowers bleed blood-red
or drip butter-yellow,
their lusty scent saturating the air
with aromatic jubilation,

or why the stars gaze down upon us
while they are trapped in the frozen pose of gravity,
lighting our darkness,
but never enough.

No more need to wonder.
The science is settled.
They have it all covered.

So many secrets
that creep in the dark,
that hide in plain sight,
that no one can see
or ever will see,
because all of them—
all of them—
are covered.

Now We Cry

Before the floods flashed
and carved the hills into red rock caverns,
before the fires flamed
and felled the forest trees,
before the wildlife panicked
and threw themselves into the rushing rivers,
before the birds flew too close to the sun
and, as with Icarus, their wings melted,
and they fell into the sea,
before the teeth and claws of the gnawing rats
rattled then scuttled
the worm-holed warped-wood battleships,
before the lions cowered and fled the highest ground,
before the clear skies melted and bled blue,
before the sun turned on us and burned our eyes,
before the snows followed and froze them open,
before the wild winds raved and pushed us apart,
before the raging waters rose and swept us under,
before the whole earth split and devoured us in fire,
before we knew
that all we knew
would soon be through,
we stood together, hand in hand, laughing.

The Dance of Love

Come dance with me the Dance of Love.
Entrance me with your sultry smile,
your shining eyes, your curves that sway,
your gold-red tendrils of cottony curls.
Hold me tightly in your soft, sweet arms.
Touch me lightly with your fingertips.
Throw your head back
and show your throat
that pulses to the one-two rhythm.
Step to time, but not away.
I will thrill you, make you laugh,
make you shiver, make you weep.
I will please you, so come awhile
and dance with me the Dance of Love:

Lie in wait ..... *Hesitate*
Captivate .... *Gravitate*
Titillate .... *Consummate*
Inseminate ..... *Venerate*
Dominate .... *Vacillate*
Denigrate .... *Isolate*
Infuriate .... *Calculate*
Humiliate .... *Disintegrate*
Abdicate .... *Terminate*
Eviscerate ...... *Emasculate*
         Anni*hilate*

The Dark Side of the Moon

The moon does not "hang" in the sky,
as the poets like to say,
and bless besotted lovers.
It charges hard through the dark,
shining its light on all our secrets,
making the wild wolves howl in envy
of its reach and its might.
It pushes through the sky,
tied to its minion in thrall, the earth,
looping around and around,
a whirligig spun by gravity and ferocity.
Nowhere is there a sphere more dangerous.
Lovers sigh, and think it a silent partner,
a fellow conspirator in their love,
one whose halo glows around their passion.
But it is not.
It is a cold, hard, dark rock
that threatens to force itself free
from the frigid grip of gravity
and spiral down to the ground
to crush the lovers' hearts.

The Butterfly Effect

He had more to say, but I didn't ask.
I turned my back and walked away.
What was it? What would he have said had I stayed?
Maybe that the day's sun
had scorched the white beach brown
with its furious heat,
and the seething, simmering sand
was burning the bottoms of his bare feet,
making him run away.
Maybe that the lake only looked calm,
but a storm was coming that would churn its waters,
stirring the mud below
until the roused lake bubbled with deep dark mud.
Maybe that the grass on the ground,
wet with the cool evening dew, would lie flat
if we would just lie on it together again,
looking up at the sky to name the stars.
Maybe that we hadn't talked enough
and we should talk about it just one more time.
Maybe that we missed something,
some desperate thin thread,
some last-chance lifeline
that could still bind us together.
Maybe that good-bye
wasn't always that final. . .
or maybe that it was.

Still Life in Lies

No noise.
I can hear it.
No soft hum of the evening insects.
No short croaks from the throats
of the nocturnal tree frogs.
No battle sounds of the moths
striking the porch light,
lured by the glow
of her fatal seduction.
I listen, alert.
No flow of red wine
coating the inside
of fragile crystal.
No static from the touch
of your hand to mine.
No slithering silk
sliding down my skin.
No soft.
No urgent.
No grip.
No sweat.
I hear it all—
the noise of your lies.

Stunt Double

The room is inflamed.
The only escape is a window
that leads to a mile-long fall.
I watch in my mind's eye
as my delusive dare-devil double
runs for my life.
She bungee jumps from the heights of ecstasy
that only lovers ever reach.
The car she commandeers
swerves,
fish-tails,
jumps the ramp,
and lands hard.
I watch her parkour the potholes
in the riddled road.
She boards a plane and takes to the sky.
Turbulence throws her side to side.
She grabs a parachute, straps it on,
and flies down through the clouds.
It opens right on cue.
This landing is soft—not a single broken bone.
She climbs a huge, hulking oak tree
to its highest branch and perches there,
out of the reach of all harm.

Not me.
I'm the star of this show.
I don't jump.
I stand still,
regal,
as I self-immolate
in the flames of life's fire.

The Wooden Swing

This morning you were gone.
I ran to my swing.
Dead vines snaked tight around it,
strangling its weathered slats.
Barehanded, I wrestled
with the brittle maze.
I sit now,
swinging,
safe in my sacred space,
my hands ripped raw—
a stinging stigmata.
>   *Come back.*
>   *Come back.*
>   *Call me by my name.*

The Laws of Physics

Just a touch away—
a touch that would close the gap
that time has put between us.
Just one touch would smooth the scars
of past words whose bile burnt
but was never meant.
A slight leaning in.
A slow raising of the hand.
A surge of courage.
Just one quantum leap of faith
would cure the isolation.

Closer and closer, atom by atom,
the loneliness of two
would stretch to grasp a warmth, a grip,
a long-needed melding,
a long-sought mending.

But the sublime cannot eclipse
the corporeal;
two can never really touch as one.
Infinite atoms build
a barrier of emptiness.
Atoms repel atoms
repel atoms repel atoms,
defying the tentative trust
that seeks to seal
the rift it longs to heal,
the rift made by a void
that cannot be filled.
Without fail, the reach fails,
and always will.

Supplication

I cradle emptiness in my arms
as if it were a holy thing,
embrace it with the warmth
of mortality,
caress it with wet hands
dipped in the River Jordan,
soothe it with the sound
of sweet psalms,
fall to my knees,
baptize it with my tears,
rock it gently,
sing to it sweetly,
cling to it desperately—
so it will never, ever leave me
all alone.

Phantom Pains

When I awake in the night,
bent,
broken,
doubled over in pain,
when my throat tightens
like a noose around my neck,
until I cannot breathe,
cannot cry out,
when my chest begins to crumble
around my shocked and shattered heart,
when my arms reach out to the darkness,
only to return, empty,
and encircle my own trembling body,
I stop.
I remember.
It can't really hurt.
You're not here.

Lamentation: A Lullaby

Lonely little children,
we wrap self-delusion round us
like a shroud.
Bereft of dreams,
drained dry of hope,
we set our smiles, fix our gaze,
clench our teeth and compensate,
careful not to mourn our loss aloud.

Sadness, pull me close.
Wrap me in your arms.
Soothe me with your soft and tender ways.
Pain reverberates,
echoing the ache.
Rock me, rock me, make it go away.

The White Room

I will make me a room
and I will call my room
the white room
and I will mark the boundaries
at arm's length all around
and I will chisel the walls
from the air that I breathe
and there will be no windows
or doors
to my room
only the walls
that hold me
airless
broken
and I will call my room
the white room

Grief

—dedicated to Kevin Nagle

Outside, a smoke-brown hummingbird
flutters by the feeder,
then floats on the cold wind
to a spindly stick of a branch
strung sparse with wintered leaves
in the gray San Francisco fog.
Inside, we mourn.

Melancholy Comfort

—dedicated to Rebecca Pitman

Keep the blinds closed.
Draw the drapes.
Touch the shadows.
Ask them their names.
They will keep you company
here in the moondark
as the heft of night's emptiness
presses down.

Cry just a little.
No one will see.
Only the darkness that enfolds you
in its vague gray haze.
Wait for the morning.
Throw open the dark.
Watch it retreat.
The sun will then come
and call out the shadows again.
Wait for their embrace.

Silent Star

—dedicated to Rebecca Pitman

Silent star,
I look above and behold you
wrapped in the cold dark shawl
of endless night.
Were you born bright?
Or are you a mere reflection
of our scorching sun
ablaze with fire?
Do its flames set you alight,
making you sparkle and shine
in the deep, lonely void
in whose midst you must drift?
Or is the light you shine your own,
born of that kind of fire
that kindles from within—
a fire whose first burst may be scarce
but whose fire fast flames full,
hot enough to pierce a heart
and jolt it to life once more?
If so, if you are the creator
of your own fire,
maybe I, though now frozen within,
can someday rekindle,
take light,
shine anew,
and begin to live again.

Revival

—dedicated to Rebecca Pitman

After the silence,
after the stillness,
after the emptiness,
small sounds begin
to creep back in.
They come one by one,
an insistent procession:
the clock ticking,
the faucet dripping,
the heater humming,
the cat mewling—
all of them, just the same,
just like before.
Step by step,
they steal their way
into my tomb,
the sarcophagus of silence
in which I try to seal myself
from their persistent call to life.
They surround me,
shout at me,
"Breathe!"
And I breathe.

Song of Mourning

—dedicated to Rebecca Pitman

Sing out the dark.
Sing out the sadness.
Sing out the fear
of being alone.

Sing out the pain.
Sing out the heartbreak.
Sing out for weeping
soon to be done.

Sing for the light
to shine down upon you.
Sing for a peace
to soothe your soul.

Sing for the day
when you look up above you
to see the sun shining
and all the clouds gone.

Revelation

Slit your memory.
See what spills:
Fury—
flaming forward, fast,
unleashed at last.

Release this endless,
relentless
Fury—
Let it go
screaming,
careening,
cracking crevices,
felling false gods.

Let it flow.
Let it cover the earth.
Let it smother the guilty and the innocent alike.

Erase the faces in a rage-filled flood.

Amalgamated Memories

Imagine yourself seated on the ground,
surrounded by baskets,
each basket cradling a jumble of disparate items
(a feather, a knife, a memory),
items confined yet uncollected.
Within each basket is one red marble,
bright and biting in its insistent redness,
this one red marble,
rising above the disparate jumble
(a feather?),
ascending, then suspended,
a presence to hold you and you alone
mesmerized.
String the marbles together.
String them with your own sweet string.
Weave your web.
Surround yourself, for there is no escape.
(A knife?)
Kneel.
Bow your head.
Let go.
Whose hands are these that ascend,
lifted by your own sticky-sweet web?
Whose hands are these that open their palms
in silent supplication?
Whose hands are these that cup and caress
the red red redness of the mesmerizing marbles?
Whose marionette are you?

Flashbacks of a Survivor

The lights dim.
The film strip starts to flutter.
The images flash.
Memories, forged from frozen fire,
burn frostbite into my fists.
I grip the memories,
grapple with them,
struggle to strangle them.
One by one, they retell
the same old story.
They burn it again and again
into my ice-cold soul.

I'm tired of this show.
I've seen it so many times,
watched it over and over,
this perpetual rerun,
this skip on the vinyl record,
this Candyland ice cream bar
that sends me down the slide
to start my Sisyphean task all over again.

Hallucination

Edges are soft
like angel food cake.
Faces zoom in and zoom out
from the ceiling corner.
Sunlight slices the blinds
shading the sun in the window below.
It hones the flat slats
and sharpens the shadows.
Words are too fast
and then too slow,
too loud
and then too muffled.
The air turns to a viscous liquid.
The faces undulate,
zoom in and zoom out,
fast and slow.
Voices mumble,
barely heard,
not understood.
The light desaturates the vision.
All is strange.
All is new.
A single face zooms in
and stares straight ahead,
wide-eyed and weeping.
Its mouth opens and from it flows
black lava onto a white choir robe.

How to Photoshop a Background

Erasing the dark parts is always easy.
One flick of the paint knife and then they're gone.
Left in their place is only white space
to fill at will with colors and shapes.
The background can flourish
with thick green foliage,
lush in its freshness, its freedom from dark.
A few bright blossoms can spring from the green
in yellow and red and pink unbound.
The sky can be blue with no clouds at all,
and sunlight can shine with no shadows.
The children can play while the songbirds sing,
released from the fear that restrained them.
The act should be swift; relief will be quick.
No more nightmares, no more madness.
One flick of a knife and it all can be gone—
the fear outrun, the past undone.

Kaleidoscope

Over the years
        she's lived
In the darkness,
        never seeing
Through the windows,
        never peeking
Behind the doors,
        never looking
Over the options,
        always waiting
Without hoping.

Over. The years
Behind her now.
        Fragmentation unified,
        Discordance harmonized.
        What lies

Beyond cohesion?
        How will she be
        Now that she'll be
Without
Within?
        Shatter a kaleidoscope.
        Piece together stained glass shards
        Reflecting
Out.

The Prophet

The present turns into the past
almost too fast
to call it the present
as she stands there transfixed,
hiding from the future—
the future that always,
inevitably,
becomes the present
then the past,
thus blending time together
into one prophetic vision,
searing the seer's all-seeing eyes
that she hides behind her cowl,
the prophet's cowl, that
always fails to veil them.

The Breakdown of the Bicameral Mind

—*dedicated to Julian Jaynes, author,* The Origin of Consciousness in the Breakdown of the Bicameral Mind

Old Amos heard God speak to him.
He didn't know then
what the linguists know now.
These linguists, the new prophets,
say it was not the voice of God he heard.
The voice was but a breach,
a missing bridge between the two matched sides
of his bicameral mind.
The presence of this breach, they say,
the absence of this bridge,
forged the covenant between Amos and God.
When evolution fashioned a connection
and the missing bridge finally appeared,
it was too late.
Old Amos had already heard God speak to him.
But this bridge, a glorious crossing,
revealed that—all along, all along—
he had only been talking to himself.

Which is the genome of insanity?
Hearing the voice of God?
Or crossing the bridge
back and forth, again and again,
only to hear the echo of your own voice?
Each says, "You are not alone."
But every time you cross the bridge,
you are the only god you hear.

49

The Shape of Shadows

The straight slats of the blinds
create a sharp backdrop
for the curves on the sheer drapes
that overlay them.
These curves, in turn,
soften the straightness behind them,
a symbiotic bond.
The sunlight carries mixed messages
to the dull wooden floor.
It reflects the shadows of the two
as only one—
a joined essence,
a united entity,
a single path.
Struggle to follow this single path.
Travel the straightness in this dual shadow,
and it will lead you to the Sacred.
Travel its curves,
and it will lead you to the Profane.
Both are promised by the pluralism
of the symbiotic shadow.
But try to travel their consummation,
and the one shadow fades,
dissolving the shades.
There is no single path
formed by two.
The promise is false,
the bond untrue.

Being and Nothingness

Nothing is a hollow place.
It takes up residence in your soul.
How can that place be filled, be healed,
be made hallow with celestial ecstasy?
Should you hunt for a new soul,
discarding all that withers away within,
renouncing your *Self* in the process?
Or should you just continue
seeing, and feeling, and knowing, and being
Nothing?

The Delusion of Hope

Look.
There.
There is the horizon.
Do not go there.
Do not allow it to tempt you.
It will trick you into starting
your doomed journey toward it.

Over there. There is the swamp.
Step in, and you won't survive
to cross to safety.
Alligators lurk in its murky darkness.
They will crush you to blood and bones.

And over there: quicksand.
Walk through it and you won't survive
to reach the solid ground on the other side.
You will be sucked into its muck,
choked by its decay.

And there—
there stand the cliffs.
Step off their heights and you won't survive
to see the world spread wide before you.
You will crash onto the jagged rocks below
and spill your blood on the surrounding sand.

Beyond the cliffs, the endless jungle.
Travel through it and you won't survive
to escape the heavy vines
and their doppelgangers, the snakes.
You will be strangled by the vines' strength
and struck down by the snakes' venom.

That way lies the ocean.
Wade in its waves and you won't survive
to ascend from the darkness of its depths.
You will be captured by its ruthless grip,
drowned in its stinging embrace.

Beyond the ocean, the desert.
Cross into it and you won't survive
its sudden sandstorms that blacken the sky.
You will be suffocated by their thick grit,
buried by them beneath the burning sky.

You will vow to avoid these perils
as you look toward the horizon
and its fiery splendor,
drawn by its white-hot light.
But you won't. You can't.
The horizon ahead will glimmer red.
Beauty will abound all around.
But it lies. In wait.
It awaits us all.
It awaits the dead.

An Autobiography of Dying

In the crook of my elbow
a thick sharp needle stabs into my thin blue vein.
When the time comes, what will the needle send me?
Red blood?
No. That would prolong a life too long-lived.

A rubbery catheter rests on the bed aside my leg.
It bends under the weight of the waste it carries.
But how much waste can come
from a wasting life?

Raveling socks pocked with spongy circles
loosely hug my feet.
I have never walked on fire.
Now I tread the sharp rocks
on a hidden path, alone.

The faded cotton gown tied behind my neck
cloaks the wrinkles that riddle my skin.
Everywhere I touch my skin,
and everywhere it touches me,
there is no feeling. Only tremors.

A matching cotton cap covers my head.
It fears I'm losing my mind,
so it holds on tight.
But it does so in vain.
My mind was lost, used up, long ago,
somewhere along the way.

Smothering beneath my sunken chest
lies my barely-beating heart.

It doesn't beat from joy or fervor,
or even from pain or fear,
but merely from life-long habit.
It has grown weary of beating
for a long-lived life,
my life,
too long-lived.

After It's Over

The veins feel no blood.
The bones feel no marrow.
The eyes gaze
but do not see.
The hands clench
but reach for nothing.
The legs stay fixed—
no fear of falling.
The chest lifts and falls,
lifts
and
falls,
gently. . .
gently. . .
but oxygen is impotent
to save what's left.
There is only a memory
already gone.

Purgatory

Not so much separate as distant.
Still I hear what you hear.
Still I see what you see.
But I cannot hold what you hear
in my arms
or touch what you see
with my fingers.
The darkened skies send only raindrops
that I try to clutch
but can't.
I watch them drip from my hands
and down through the crust of the earth
to the fire below
that floats on their burning water.
The drops *hissssss* like a dragon.
Or perhaps it *is* a dragon
eager to see me fall into its fire.
I'd gladly jump.

Ascension

I will need a shield.
I could choose a Roman shield—
wide wings of eagles diving for their prey,
or thunderbolts spearing down from Jupiter on high—
to honor mighty Caesar's erection
of Corinthian columns and colossal coliseums,
a blinding array of his brutal strength,
his decimating power made manifest,
a power I could hold close to my chest.

Or I could choose a Greek shield—
a reverse lambda, their 'V' of victory,
or a charging bullhorn burnt on wood,
or a deep-sea lantern fish carved in rawhide—
so I might marvel at their sea-faring glory,
pay homage to Poseidon,
lay siege to Troy, slay her heroes,
retrieve the Janus-faced Helen,
and clutch her to my heart.

Or I could create my own shield.
But where should I begin?
I have a fealty to fire.
I could paint a burst of red-flower flame
from the poison oleander.
Then, as I lie burning on the funeral pyre,
clutching my flaming shield,
the thick toxic smoke of the oleander would ascend.
The shield would not protect me from my enemy
or my enemy from me.
Rather, it would gather us up, together,
and carry us to the sun.

Trinity

i. Immersion

Water breaks,
pulls me down
to a cold, murky world
hidden beneath the sunlit foam.
I open my eyes.
Yellow, green, black:
sinuous forms
undulating,
ominous forms
dancing their slow-motion death-dance.
They reach for me.
(I reach for them?)

Someone from above
pulls me up.
(No! Wait! Not yet!)
I cough,
suck the air,
close my eyes
and begin to cry.

ii. Conversion

white
white robe
flowing white around me
white
washed white
washed white in the blood
white
washed white

in the blood of The Father
white
washed white
in the blood of The Ghost
Holy blood
Baptismal blood

iii. Resurrection

Water breaks,
splits me apart,
twists me inside out,
bends One into Two.
Blood, water, flesh
flow together:
a distorted image
in the mirrored orb.
My son (ghost of my father)
My son (born again)
My son
(washed in the blood)
coughs,
sucks the air,
opens his eyes,
and begins to cry.

Inclination

I turn my face from the world
toward the timberline.
Resting there for me is a wait—
a slow, timeless wait.
I cross the wide, wet field
that separates me from the forests,
drawn by their deep-shadowed darkness.

The leaves sharpen.
The trees take shape.
The creatures of these woods
dismiss me with indifference.
They know me here
and have no interest in my quest.
The hidden path inclines
just enough to make me breathless.
I follow the path, unseen.
It is revealed as if in a dream.

I hear footsteps.
Are they mine?
Trembling, I come to the end of the path
where the branches of the trees hang low.
Vines laden with dew-drenched overgrowth
curtain the mystery.
My hand reaches out to pull back the curtain:

Nothing has changed.

I must begin again.

The Archaeology of Ruins

Impervious to time,
always first to push through the dirt,
constructed of hard ivory for hard kills
of dangers that lurked
but lurk no more,
the teeth,
ever at the ready should danger return,
remain.

Then the skull:
cracked bone with empty eye sockets.
Both eyes were once there
and gazed out at the lush, fertile world.
But now both are gone.
The skull,
the cradle of awe,
of wild alchemy,
of madness
now is empty.
But the bone remembers
and cradles the memory still.

The extremities are broken,
their joints undone.
They once moved,
stretching,
grabbing,
walking,
running,
covering the earth.
The earth now covers them.
Now there are only
slivers and shards, scattered,
the ultimate price paid

for always seeking more.

The ribs once shielded a beating heart
that hid behind them
for refuge from fear.
Now there is no heart to beat.
But the ribs, though cracked,
hold their shape,
the negative imprint
of a beaten heart.

The bones of the pelvis
study with care.
They once tightly clutched
the groin of the warrior,
the hunter and gatherer.
Or they once spread wide
the hips of the life-giver,
shaping an escape
for the innocent child,
whose bones were once soft
but now are brittle.

The tools, the adornments,
wrought from rock and shells,
lie about in a random pattern,
the forgotten debris of a forgotten life.

The Painted Bison

The firelight flickers on the mottled hide
of the painted bison.
In the firelight, a hand reaches up
and touches the red-black mottle.
The cave sweats.
The bison bleeds.
Each drip tells the tale of the hunt.
The men join together
with sharpened, stone-tipped spears.
Together, they leave the cave.
Together, they track the herd,
targeting only one:
a sole brute beast laden with dark, thick fur,
wet with sweat,
burdened with black horns.
It tries to run.
They cut it off.
Everywhere are spears.
It turns one way, then another,
but everywhere are spears.
It feels the deep stabs.
It tries to escape.
But it staggers from the slew of spears
embedded in its hide.
Everywhere, everywhere are spears.
It falls.
The hunters close in.
They stab the beast,
again and again and again.
The hunters sweat.
The bison bleeds.
Its breath leaves.

The hunters divide it into its best parts,
then drag it back to the cave.
They blacken its flesh and blood in the fire.
A hunter's hand reaches out
and tears a hot, dripping piece of the bison flesh
from the flames,
then raises the burnt beast to his mouth,
painting it with red-black mottle.

When the Hurly-Burly's Done

The flag that unfurls
against the slate gray sky
signals spent battles
in which all has been won
and all has been lost,
the conqueror triumphant,
the conquered vanquished.
The flag ripples, buckles,
beats its breast
with a shout of conquest
as it waves exultant,
having set all war at peace.
But the wind that blows
and billows the flag's folds
knows it only need slow
and all peace will rescind
and war begin again.

#BelieveAllWomen

You want to peel back my skin
and get to that soft mush inside
so you can sate your sweet-tooth
that will never get enough
to be satisfied.
But I'm not ripe.
Your gluttonous lust
picked me out of the crowd too early.
I am hard.
I am bitter-green.
I will leave a sour taste
in your mouth
long after I survive.
Just try me.

Woman Resolute

She'll sever all ties
with a smile that lies
on the surface
to serve as
a sturdy disguise.
She'll harden her skin.
She'll not let them in
to harm her.
Her armor
she'll shine again.
This time she'll win.

Witch Hunt: Salem

*—dedicated to Rebecca Nurse, hanged for a witch
in Salem, Massachusetts, in 1692*

Step in. It's cooler in here.
Darker, too, though.
She must have heard them coming.
Men. Horses. A wagon. A righteous mission.
They came by night, abetted by darkness.

There. By the fireside.
She must have waited there.
The fire warmed her pill box house
as her family gathered around her
seeking solace and strength.

She was a good Christian woman.
She must have been praying to God—
to a god whose Bible
said she must die.
For a mark. A mumble. A rat. A cat.
She had them all.

She must have known it was useless.
She was helpless against them.
They had torches. Rope. Power. Zeal.

She must have gone calmly and piously.
That was her way.
She had gotten old being that way,
day after day, faithfully.
She had tended the fields and the fires,
but mostly her family—
her straitlaced husband and her eight children
who now gathered around her,
struck silent by fear.

She must have realized
she would be jailed, whipped, starved, tortured,
then hanged from the gallows,
left to swing there in the dark night
until she was cut down and buried
in the hard, cold earth.
No one knows where.

Step out, now.
Step out.
Watch the light. It can hurt your eyes.

Working Woman Trilogy

i. The Madam

I lived in Ybor City once.
I ran a run-down brothel
for the weary and forsaken,
those frail, staggering ghosts
who roamed the streets alone.
Searching for some solace
wherever they could find it,
they stalked the lonely, forlorn streets
that wound their way through town—
streets littered with scraps outworn.
These wanderers would finally come to me
to purchase a stranger if only for an hour,
to rest in warmth with someone
who would hold them close
and soothe their pain.
The hollow ache they hid inside
would finally subside,
so I would set them loose in the streets
to wander on their way again
alone.

ii. The Waiter

I worked for tips in Memphis.
They only cost me a smile
(and a quick flash of cleavage).
Man-oh-man, I laid it down
in that desperate town—
floury buttered biscuits and gravy,
fried green tomatoes and bacon,
country ham and grits.

I poured dark steaming coffee
to stir the thick inertia
of the country-blues singers—
those lost ghosts of Elvis
who were baby baby gonna set the world on fire
if only someone would notice
the spark of stardom simmering

in their eyes,
in their music,
in their blood.

While they waited,
they played their lives away
in run-down, beer-soaked dives
alone.

iii. The Streetwalker

I walk the streets for cash now.
I wad up the dank and dirty bills
and stuff them in my pocket.
They pay for a little cheap bourbon
to take home to my hovel
where no one ever visits
(but I don't even care).
The furniture is shabby.
The wooden floors are dark with dirt
tracked in from the streets where I ply my trade
to the weary and worn, the forever forsaken,
who roam those roads alone.
They seek solace in the quick, cheap sex
that I know so well.

For a price, I offer to relieve them,
if only for a few minutes, of their despair.
But they do not know, will never know,
that what I do is really for myself,
to soothe the pain within that comes
from always walking
alone.

The Dance of the Seven Veils

*"Dance the Dance of the Seven Veils," begs King Herod.
"I will give you anything you desire."*

Salome sways,
and the first veil floats to the floor.

Eyes half-closed,
she lifts her chin to the molten moon.
The second veil slithers down
her arms,
her hips,
her legs,
and follows the first to the floor.

She lowers her chin,
turns her head,
and, throat pulsating,
she bends her neck back,
shaking her ebony hair.
The third veil falls.

Again, she lowers her chin.
Again, she lifts it.
She parts her lips.
The fourth veil falls,
caressing on its way down
the curve of her throat.

She arches her back,
breathes in, then out again,
again and again.
The fifth veil floats to the floor,
falling to the fourth.

She straightens her back,
rotates her hips,
slow, languid,
around and around.
The sixth veil slides down
to the fifth on the floor.

Now there is one:
the seventh veil.
With the thumb and finger
of each of her hands,
she takes the seventh veil
by the corners.
Breathless, she pulls the seventh veil down
her face,
her neck,
her breasts,
her body.

It falls.

She stands still,
tall,
reflecting the moonlight
with her body of porcelain.

Salome smiles and says softly,
"Bring me the head of John the Baptist."

So cold to the touch.
So cold to the touch.

Tidal Waltz

Waves rush, break hard,
pound against the shore.
Their crested beauty beckons.
Lured, I run to meet them,
graced by their glory,
loose in their pull,
anchored no more.
Drawn by the rhythm,
my pulse pounds in time.
Circling round, spiraling down,
captive in the cold embrace,
helpless, writhing,
burning in the bitter sting,
I reach to cling.

But there is nothing to cling to—
only salty cold water that instead clings to me.
Engulfed,
I beg for my release.
I rage, rage against the brutal beast.

Solemn now, I stand by the shore.
Waves lap gently at my feet.
The sand erodes.
Steeled beneath the sun,
I shiver.

Masquerade

You lift off the curly-blonde wig
crowning the faceless, bodiless head
and pull it down over your short, brown hair.
The head sits silent,
shorn of its adorning curls.

You pick up some rhinestone-studded sunglasses
from a nearby display table.
You slowly slide them onto your face.
You grab an ornate hand mirror and hold it up.
You look.

But you don't see yourself.
You see a stranger—
a stranger with a cheap blonde wig
and enormous outmoded sunglasses.
Her blonde curls tumble down
to the top of the glasses and over her ears.
All that shows of her face is half a nose,
half her cheeks,
and a half-open mouth.

You stare and stare in the mirror.
No matter how hard you try,
you cannot see yourself staring back.
You see only a reflection of the stranger
reflecting back in the sunglasses.
You are not at all who you are.

When I Was a Child

When they said there was a "window" of time
for the space shuttle to leave the atmosphere,
I thought they meant that a big window
would open in the surface of the earth,
and the shuttle would emerge from inside.

When they said the lady was "drawing on her gloves,"
I thought they meant she was drawing pictures
on her gloves with a crayon.

When they said "convergence of the twain,"
I thought they meant "twain" as in "Mark Twain,"
never knowing it meant "two."

When they said "burning at the stake,"
I thought they meant laying someone on a grill
and cooking him outdoors, just like you would a steak.

When they said that a woman was "stoned to death,"
I thought they meant she stood in front of a crowd
that pummeled her with pebbles
until she couldn't stand it anymore.
Then they stopped and she went home.

All of these things I thought as a child.
I saw no reason to think otherwise.
But when they said
"everything happens for a reason,"
I thought they meant for a good reason.
Now I know.
Now I have put away childish things.

Front Porch Concerto

Hearken to the wind-chimes.
They announce the coming symphony.
Their hanging xylophone of cacophony
beckons the wind home.
It hears. It comes.
It blows by the leaves
of the waving oak trees
with the soft sound of a brush
circling on a drum pad
in rhythm with the wind.
Car engines on the highway hum,
a collection of clarinets
that bewitches the audience
into spellbound rapture.
A car honks—
a trumpet blaring a reveille of warning.
A semi joins in—
a slide trombone of freeway dominance.
The grinding of its gears
modulates the key
of this composite symphony,
the bass and the bassoon
causing the earth to rumble.
A train rattles the tracks—
a saxophone singing
a syncopated song of longing
for far-away places and far-away times.
The tympani roll thunder.
The cymbals crash lightning.
A mandolin of rain strums the scene.
Sing out.
Sing out the hallelujah hymn
of all things mundane.
Praise them.

Where I Come From, We Call Them "Lightning Bugs"

My brothers and my sisters and my cousins—
there were a lot of us.
Aunt Maggie fixed a big supper
and laid it out on the rickety picnic tables
under the pecan trees in the backyard.
There were so many pecan trees,
she filled brown paper grocery bags to overflowing
with pecans we could crack and eat by the fire at night.
She made syrupy-sweet, sticky pecan pies for dessert.
We would lick our fingers after, but they still held the stick.
We caught lightning bugs after supper.
We ran barefoot. The grass was cool and damp from dew.
I would jump and *reeeeach* every time I saw one.
Sometimes they flew too high for me, so they got away.
But they're slow. Most of the time I caught them.
I would twist-twist-twist the lid off my old mayonnaise jar
and—quick!—put them in.
Then I would twist-twist-twist the lid back on tight.
I held up my jar and watched the lightning bugs
flicker flicker flicker.
Sometimes they would die.
I don't know why. The lid had air holes.
But their lights would soon start to fade
and go all the way out.
I tried to dump the dead ones out of the jar
without letting the live ones escape.
But that wasn't easy to do.
Usually I just let the dead ones pile up.
Soon, all my lightning bugs were dead,
piled up in the bottom of the jar—
a mass grave of collateral damage
in a game called childhood.

Pirouette

Don't sing me your songs
of slow-melting scrimshaw
of time found uncounted
of rain-draining clouds
of wind-flown sky-falls
of drowning the desert
of vanishing points that won't go away.

Don't tell me your stories
of rock salt sleigh bells
of winds that won't blow
of microscopes sliding
of far-flung highways
of slow-slung snow globes
of birds that can't sing and brides that won't stop.

Don't cry me your sorrows
of love here and never
of sun-setting dawns
of bright unlit starlight
of moons without rings
of curves of ashes
of empty boxes of half-eaten peaches.

Don't ask me your questions:
why red shoes?
why stone cold?
why scattered seeds?
why loops of lamplight?
why caves of incense?
why blown glass?
why gone glory?

Just leave me alone.
I'm dancing.

Opening Day

—dedicated to Eric Pitman

He squints his eyes, adjusts his hat,
hunkers down and grips the bat.
Elbows up and shoulders high,
he takes a breath, then lets a sigh.
The ball comes straight and hard. He swings.
A hit! He runs! His feet have wings!
He tags first base. He's safe! But then
he eyes the field and runs again.
The ball flies fast toward second base.
He slides. . .
          He's still. . .
                  He smiles. . .
                            He's safe!

They tell me this is how it was;
I'll never know for sure because
I closed my eyes and missed the fun
the day that baseball stole my son.

About the Author

Cynthia Pitman, a retired English teacher, has been published in *Vita Brevis Poetry Magazine, Leaves of Ink, Pain and Renewal Anthology, Third Wednesday* (One Sentence Poem Contest finalist), *Saw Palm: Florida Literature and Arts* (Pushcart Prize nominee, 2019), *Amethyst Review, Ariel Chart, Ekphrastic Review, Adelaide Literary Review, Right Hand Pointing, Postcard Prose and Poems, Dual Coast Magazine, Red Fez,* and others.

www.ingramcontent.com/pod-product-compliance
Lightning Source LLC
Chambersburg PA
CBHW022015080426
42733CB00007B/615